It's the Principle
of the Thing

It's the Principle of the Thing

DON H. STAHELI

SHADOW
MOUNTAIN

Library of Congress Cataloging-in-Publication Data

Staheli, Don H.
  It's the principle of the thing / Don H. Staheli.
      p.   cm.
    ISBN 1-57008-873-X (pbk.)
    1. Conduct of life.   I. Title: It's the principle of the thing.
  II. Title.
    BJ1581.2724 2002
    248.4—dc21   2002007732

Printed in the United States of America   7973-6662
Bang Printing, Brainerd, MN

10   9   8   7   6   5   4   3   2   1

To my sweet wife, wonderful children,
dear mom and dad, and all who
have given me eyes to see

Contents

Acknowledgments

I am deeply grateful to Sheri Dew and Emily Watts of Shadow Mountain, and to the other incredible people who in sharing a moment or two of their lives have greatly enriched mine. Special thanks to Cyndy for her love and encouragement.

Introduction

In a conversation I was having with a delightful young lady, when I asked her to tell me a little about herself, she replied immediately, "I have a very interesting history, even though I'm only twenty-one!"

How true! We all have a most interesting story to tell, regardless of our age. Our two-year-old granddaughter is thrilled to tell us what she has been doing, what she has seen, heard, and experienced. She is learning so much. A twenty-year-old has ten times the stories to tell! And an eighty-year-old four times as many as that!

Every day, all of us, if we will just pay attention, are taught over and over again the lessons of life. We miss most of what life has to offer by way of education simply because we're pulling the same tricks now as we have through much of our schooling—we're daydreaming, gawking at somebody, or so worried about ourselves and how other people perceive us that our own perception is stymied.

This little collection is a small sampling of experiences to which I have actually paid attention. They aren't particularly different from yours. As you read them, you'll probably remember when life tried to teach you the same principles.

When the memory of details fades and you really can't recall exactly what went on or why it happened, the principle of the thing will endure in your mind.

1

The Target

As a young military officer, I wanted desperately to win a ribbon to pin in the empty space above the name tag on my uniform. It seemed like I was the only one on the base who didn't have a splash of color on his chest. Most had several ribbons, and a few had so many that they appeared a little slant-shouldered as they walked. They were loaded down with honor. All I had was a plastic name tag.

I didn't mind the military. My father was a career Navy man, and I had more or less grown up in the environment. Plenty of patriotism in our family. I found no joy, however, in the rank of second lieutenant. My French instruction had taught that *lieu* means place and that *tenant* means holding. Why, a lieutenant was nothing more than a placeholder, someone to take up space. In math the placeholder is the zero! So there you have it: I was a military zero without a ribbon to my name.

I was learning to cope with the relative ignominy of being a second lieutenant, but a chest naked of ribbons was almost too much to bear. The young enlisted men and women, a few ribbons earned in basic training proudly displayed on their uniforms, would salute me when they had to, but I was pretty sure I could see their eyes dart quickly to my bare chest as if it were a gaping wound—a sickening sight, politely ignored.

The day came when I had a chance to earn a ribbon, but my hopes were not too high. The training exercise was pistol shooting. Unfortunately, only those who hit the target with expert proficiency would win the right to wear the marksman ribbon.

I had shot a pistol only once before and couldn't hit the proverbial broad side of a barn. The barrel of the gun seemed to waver in almost uncontrollable fashion. Every breath or blink of the eyes sent it off in another direction, always away from the tin can or whatever target it was my intention to hit. My only chance to win this ribbon lay in listening carefully to the expert instructor, applying everything he suggested, and hoping for the best.

The first thing he taught us was how to hold the pistol so it would be more steady in our hands. *Good,* I thought, *I can do that. It will help. Maybe I can hit the target!*

The next thing he said made very little sense and replaced my budding confidence with confusion. His statement went against every notion I had practiced as a child when it came to hitting something with a projectile of whatever kind, be it a snowball, a rock, or a ball. The instructor said, "If you can see the target, you won't hit it!"

What? How am I supposed to hit it, if I can't see it? What kind of an expert is this guy, anyhow? Well, he's the kind of expert who has a lot of ribbons on his chest, so maybe I'd better listen and figure out what he is trying to tell us.

The instructor went on to explain the obvious fact that our eyes can't focus on two separate objects at the same time, if one of the objects is close and the other is distant. Try it! Try focusing on the words on this page and, at the same time, on the picture on the wall across the room. See, it really can't be done. You can kind of see both at once, but you can't focus on both at the same time. The sights of the pistol, when held at arm's length, were only a couple of feet from my eyes. The target, on the other hand, was some fifty feet or more away. Impossible to focus on both at once.

It seemed a natural inclination to pay greatest attention to the object of my aim—the target. But if I focused my eyes on the target, then the sights of the gun were blurry and could not be aligned well enough to make a good shot. The pistol may be steady, we might have the target well in mind and know exactly what we want to hit, but if the sights are not properly focused, the shot will go awry. We'll miss the bull's-eye. No ribbon.

The solution to this dilemma was surprisingly simple. We young officers were instructed to first look forward down the barrel of the pistol and focus on the target. It is important to know what we want to hit, what we want to achieve. We have to know where the bull's-eye is!

When we felt comfortable with the target, then our eyes could be focused on the sights of the pistol, not far from the end of our nose. It was vital that the sights be clearly in focus and aligned just right when the gun discharged, sending the projectile toward the target.

In living, it seems we too often focus well on the distant goal, but forget to take care of the here and now. We think we know where we want to go, but we are unwilling or unable to line things up correctly so we will end up there.

For example, all of us want a comfortable retirement, but few are willing to be disciplined, to align their current finances so the rosy target can be realized down the road. Most people want a successful career, but many are unwilling to line up their education and training so they can one day hit the bull's-eye of satisfying work. We want our children to be happy, responsible adults, but we often fail to nurture and teach them early on in their youth.

I think everybody wants to go to his or her notion of heaven, but only a few seem interested in doing what it takes today to achieve that kind of seemingly distant tomorrow. Too much focus on the target, not enough attention paid to the task at hand. And if you can see the target, you won't hit it.

So, we must first get a vision of the target, understand our goal and what results we want for our effort. We must have a good understanding of the direction we want things to go.

Second, we should focus on that which is right in front of us. We must pay attention to the tasks within our immediate reach. They have to be done right. Then, when we pull the trigger, all the power will be pointed in the direction we want it to go. The bullet will take care of itself and will hit the target.

It works! In my very short military career, it was the only ribbon I won.

When we pay close attention to
the small things in life, the big
things have a way of taking care
of themselves.

②

Life in Smallville

With mixed emotions our family received the announcement that a work transfer would take us to a small town in southeastern Utah. We were living in northern San Diego County at the time, and it seemed that we were going from a semitropical paradise to a dry wasteland of sagebrush and dirt. Besides that, the biggest store in this little town would easily fit into one floor of the huge department store down at the mall. The nearest "civilization" was eighty miles away over a treacherous mountain pass, and "blue collar" best described the most prevalent forms of entertainment.

Our fears were only worsened by a supposedly well-meaning friend who somehow knew about this town. He likened it to various unattractive parts of the human anatomy and said it was the one place only a fool would go. Thanks for the encouragement!

Wasteland, isolation, and a cultureless society without malls. It sounded like a bad place to live. But loyalty, and a desire to keep bread on the table, motivated us to pack up the station wagon and wave good-bye to palm trees, gentle sea breezes, and California gentility for a trip into no-man's-land. We took our time getting there.

Our first night in Smallville was no great introduction. We slept in a run-down motel with walls only a bit more thick than the paint. No cable TV. It didn't exist in that area. Only the McDonald's restaurant seemed familiar, so we spent a lot of time there.

We moved into a nice enough home in a newer subdivision, and it didn't take long before the neighbors began to come over to introduce themselves and welcome us into their community. These were extraordinarily good people. They were well-educated or skilled in their professions. They laughed easily and seemed content, not deprived of the necessities of life. They brought hot loaves of bread and plates of cookies and offered to assist in any way we might need. Their children asked ours to come out and play and soon they had a great fort built in the backyard out of packing boxes and old lumber. We weren't meeting the fools about which our friend had warned us.

Admittedly, there was no evidence of the kind of culture we had enjoyed in southern California. The only plays we saw were at the high school. The best jazz band in town was made up of junior high kids. The orchestra was directed by a local guy who taught at the junior college, a struggling institution of only somewhat higher education and no football team.

But wait a minute. Our oldest daughter played the lead in some of those high school plays. She was great! Our son wailed on his trumpet and learned to play some wonderful jazz pieces. My wife and I joined a group of singers and had a tremendous time vocalizing, even with the accompaniment of the orchestra on one occasion. It seemed all of our children and many of the neighbors were sharing their talents, making their own culture and really entertaining one another. This was a great place to be!

The gatherings in people's homes or down at the church were the most fun. We had little else to do for night life, so we got together and played.

One Saturday, some enterprising souls transformed the recreation hall at the church into a replica of an elegant hotel lobby. Where had they found all that stuff? It looked like downtown Chicago. There was a huge front desk, a bank of key boxes complete with room keys, and couches and chairs and lamps.

Several classrooms in the church were decorated with posters and trinkets depicting a particular country, be it France or Mexico or England. When couples entered the hall and "checked in" at the front desk, they were assigned to a particular classroom for dinner. Volunteers recruited by the organizers were busy in the church kitchen serving up several different dinner menus to be enjoyed in the classroom-dining room decorated to match the ethnic cuisine. In the room with the Eiffel Tower poster, we had a wonderful meal of French onion soup and all the trimmings. As I recall, there was some sort of flaming dessert (topped with vanilla, I suppose, since liquor wasn't necessary to make these get-togethers fun).

After dinner, we pushed back the couches and chairs in the "lobby" and a local group of '60s-rock-band wannabes came in to really liven up the place. We danced, or watched as others did, to tunes we all remembered and enjoyed. I almost asked to step up to the mike when my favorite Beach Boys song was played. I wasn't foolish enough to really try it, but I'm certain they would have welcomed me and cheered my effort, even if I cracked on the high notes. They were that kind of people. They were friends.

Well, we lived, really lived, in that little town for about nine years. Our kids pretty much grew up there. In that amount of time, the successful development of local industries strengthened the economy and caused new, larger stores to be built. The junior college more than doubled in size, and it was offering a very good educational experience and sending well-prepared students off to the university. The once meager holiday parade down Main Street even attracted a gaggle of Shriner clowns from the big city over the mountain. What more could you ask for?

When we were again transferred and had to leave our home, the roots were tough to pull up. I think some of them still remain in that sagebrush-covered dirt. A large part of our hearts and many of our most cherished memories are there.

I suppose it was a bad place to live. But it was a great place to be.

Happiness doesn't depend on where you are, it depends on how you are.

③

Song of the Bird

Sometimes girls are the strongest of all. My youngest daughter came home from school one day proudly proclaiming herself the arm-wrestling champion of the second grade. Strongest? No question about it. With a grasp that resembled a death grip, and a look of fierce determination on her face, she had struggled to put down the hand of each antagonist, forcing them to an ignominious acknowledgment of her superior physical strength. In other words, she had whupped every one of the kids who had dared to put an elbow to the desktop.

Really, there weren't very many challengers. Once she beat the first, only a few who were stupid or overconfident, or both, were willing to step forward. Sometimes champions remain such mostly because no one questions their supremacy. It didn't matter to her, nor should it have. She reigned victorious then and isn't easy to beat even now.

But I guess the strongest girl I ever saw was actually pretty frail and would have been no match in an arm-wrestling contest. In fact, her memories of second grade are somewhat blurred and tend to be void of notable successes. Mostly she remembers fear, confusion, and a deep self-loathing. It was during this time of her life that she was being abused by her stepfather.

Millie (of course, that is not her real name) was physically and sexually abused by her mother's second husband. He was not a nice guy, but we will leave his punishment to the powers that be. Millie isn't interested in punishing anybody. She knows what pain is like and doesn't want to be involved in giving or receiving any more of it.

When I met Millie, she was a young woman trying to understand what she had done to deserve such treatment. In her confused and painful thinking, she was certain that he wouldn't have done it without some provocation or enticement. He had told her it was her fault. And grown-ups are always right, aren't they?

But Millie was strong. Even with that misplaced sense of responsibility for her traumatic circumstances, she was trying to fight her way out. She was trying to figure out how to live with the memory of the abuse and not be consumed by it.

Millie worked very hard to put her experience into proper perspective, to comprehend the true innocence of youth, and to assign blame to the real culprit. For some time, the best she was able to do was to label herself a victim. This was an important first step, realizing that she had been victimized and that it wasn't her fault, but for Millie it wasn't enough. She wanted freedom from the ongoing victimization of the terrible experience. She wanted to somehow let go of it completely.

In her quest for peace, Millie was able to come to a realization that (1) what happened to her was wrong, (2) it was not her fault, and (3) it didn't need to happen again, ever. That was actually pretty easy for her to figure out and to accept. She could see now that he was more physically powerful than she and that her ability to resist was minimal. It was not too difficult for Millie to place the blame where it belonged and to lose her fear that something like this would happen to her again. That was mostly an intellectual exercise. Those conclusions were quite logical.

It was harder for Millie to deal with the feeling that she was "damaged goods." Even though feeling less to blame, she still felt dirty, a little crazy, and a bit out of control.

One day Millie was stunned by a thought-provoking passage from Victor Hugo's *Les Miserables*. She read, "The soul helps the body and at certain moments uplifts it. It is the only bird that sustains its cage."

Wait a minute! You mean there is a difference between the soul and the body? Do you mean to tell me that my body is sort of like a cage that surrounds the real me? If that is so, then could it be that he was hurting the cage, but that the bird was not damaged at all?

Of course! He could beat the cage, he could abuse the cage, he could even break the cage, but he couldn't get at the beautiful bird inside. Even if he destroyed the cage, the bird would just fly free, beyond his ability to inflict any harm. He might frighten the little bird out of singing for a while, but he could not take away her song forever.

With this insight, Millie was liberated. She began to comprehend her dual identity. She started to understand that there is the Millie we all see, the one who moves about us—the "cage." But there is also the Millie who dwells inside, out of sight, and is real, alive and powerful—the "bird." Her stepfather may have been able to hurt her body, but the inside Millie is still clean and whole, with a beautiful song to sing.

Millie stopped calling herself a victim. No more labels. She ceased defining herself by what he had done to her. The abuse is something that happened *to* her, it is not *her*.

Millie is the strongest person I have ever met. Even though her cage may have been bruised, battered, and a little broken, she can still sing, like a bird, the beautiful songs of peace and love.

Bad things may happen to me,
but they are not me.

Climbing Trees

What is there about a tree that makes a young person crave to climb it? I guess even we older people want to climb, but the yearning is rarely powerful enough to entice us into the branches. All I can remember about the last time I climbed a tree is how long it took to get the sap off of my hands. Children don't worry about sap.

And tree climbing is definitely a lot more than just hefting oneself up over a branch or two. Oh, yes, real tree climbing is both an art and a science. True mastery is achieved only when one possesses an acute sensitivity to the subtle nuances of arboreal ascension.

The scientific aspects were clearly demonstrated to a group of us youthful climbers engaged in the doubles form of the game. We lived near a large tract of trees, both hardwoods and evergreens in varying stages of development. The springy young pine trees were the object of our interest on many an expedition into this adventureland with which, we were sure, even Tarzan would have been intrigued.

Each tree to be climbed was chosen with great care—not too big and not too small, with just the right amount of spring. Two boys to a tree. The first one up the limbs went as high as he could with the other boy in pursuit. As the second came close to the top of the tree, their combined weight would cause it to bend slowly downward, bending farther and farther, until the upper trunk had dipped its occupants down to a safe distance from the ground. Their four feet dangling a short way above Mother Earth, the boys prepared to drop from the tree. With the fortitude of all young fliers (any landing you can walk away from is a good one), they were ready to yield to gravity and hope for a kind reception on the unyielding turf. Physics at its finest.

Now, the artistry of the effort was manifest in

the split-second timing of the release. With synchronicity usually reserved for a far more sophisticated setting, the two boys, acting as one, released their grip on the sappy limbs. The well-torqued trunk sprang like an unloaded catapult back to upright dignity. The boys dropped to the ground with hardly a thud, their reward the cheers of admiring peers, each of whom judged the feat a 10. What fun! Find another perfect tree and go for it again.

In one particularly exciting bout, the smallest of our crew headed up a young pine. He had to be matched with the heaviest boy among us in order to create a combined weight adequate to bend the tree. Sure enough, they moved toward the summit and the tree bowed to their wishes. All was going well. The tree lowered to a proper height, hands let go, and up sprang the tree. But this time only two feet hit the ground. The heavy boy had let go before the light one was ready. Our little buddy nearly cracked like a whip as he shot up with the treetop. The snap of the tree shook him loose, and down he tumbled through the branches. Two broken arms and a stern parental lecture later, our tandem tree climbing had to be put on hold for a while.

The older we get, the more obvious it is to us that we should stay out of trees. A guy can get hurt! But we sure do a lot of other things without thinking too much about the consequences. We may not exactly be scaling the oaks, but we introduce plenty of risk into our lives. We drive too fast, we go too far into debt, we eat too much junk food, we take on too much stress. Most of us, in one way or another, are way out on a limb, never figuring that something will go wrong. None of us young tree climbers ever thought about the possibility of broken arms, either. Our friend learned the lesson the hard way!

Never climb higher than you're willing to fall.

(5)

Connections

With flowers in hand, we walk quietly through the small town cemetery, a little flock of reverent pilgrims come to decorate the graves of loved ones long gone but kept alive through faith and fond memories. Though we have come early, others have been there before us, and most of the stone-grey headstones are brightened with colorful memorials to cherished companionships and treasured heritage. In such a place, we pick our way carefully, unable to completely put away the thought that somehow those who rest in peace are just a little disturbed by footfalls on the grass.

As we stand at great-grandma's grave, someone thinks to figure the levels of lineage represented here, and all are struck by the fact that combined above and below the ground are six generations.

Represented by marker or lively presence is a pedigree that spans the age from settlers to space travelers, from bonnets to backwards baseball caps. In coming to this hallowed ground, we think of those who may hardly have imagined us and our times; searching for the parts of them that still live in us, we feel connected. We are connected by means of genes and history and, in the graveyard near their hometown, even a physical proximity.

This feeling of connectedness, of belonging, seems to be the yearning of every human heart from the first beat to the last. From the moment the umbilical cord is severed and we are disconnected from our mothers, we spend our entire lives trying to reconnect with people and enjoy again the sense of bonding that characterized that closest of all human relationships. As death approaches, the worst fear may be that we will die alone, without the comfort of a loving escort to keep us feeling connected to humanity until the very end.

Even the hard-core loner wants on occasion to feel he belongs, or at least to be linked with a listening ear. Unfortunately, some have felt their only voice was some harmful act directed at those who might well have made the connection had they understood the need. For those who lose all sense of affiliation, the very purpose of life may be lost in plain sight. Suicide becomes an act of emotional blindness, as its victims ignore the connecting ties that would keep them from falling if only they could see them.

We may not label ourselves as "joiners," but each of us is such, in our effort to be connected. Children naturally cling to the apron strings, and separation anxiety seems common to nearly all. Young people are drawn by an almost irresistible force to connect with those of their own age. Wearing the right clothes in the right place with the right people can become more important than doing the right thing. Even those who want to be "different" often do so by joining others with similar tastes in style and thought. In such cases, loneliness is sometimes the only real link.

The most successful companies help their employees feel connected to the mission of the firm and refer to the workers as "family" or at least "associates." We wear logos and sport the right colors so we can feel like a part of the team. We research our family history and correct those who mispronounce our surnames because we want to feel rightly connected.

There is some danger in this drive for connectedness. Some of us will seek to belong in ways that can be destructive. Disconnected youth join gangs, which give them a sense of acceptance and invulnerability. But condemnation by the criminal justice system shatters the tenuous bonds of neighborhood gang membership, and puts the now highly vulnerable young inmate into a precarious circumstance that forces connection with those who would use and abuse as the price of protection.

People who lack the warmth of loving relationships may settle for a perverted form in promiscuous behavior that yields only a momentary sense of being nurtured. Subsequent abandonment will only heighten the need to stay connected at any cost, even the sacrifice of self-respect.

Compare these faulty forms of pseudoconnectedness with the permanent bonds that not only last but lift and strengthen. Usually the bonds of family are the strongest of all. Such connections pass to us the legacy of love we hold for those we may have never known, but who continue as an important part of who we are now. Those through whom I am descended have passed to me a firmness of faith, a willingness to pioneer and persevere, and a desire to hand down to my descendants a history of integrity and service like the one I received. In order to insure future connections, my life must provide the fuel of love and learning needed to maintain the energy that will power the next generation. That generation will then have the ability to start the next, and so on, as the links are held intact. Happily, in this process there is plenty of room for variety in individual application. We can revel in our uniqueness while still appreciating our heritage.

Even one generation gone seriously awry can create a momentum in inherited dysfunctional lifestyle that is changed only through uncommon self-awareness and determination on the part of some victim-heir. Greater courage hardly exists than that required of the one who recognizes family deficits and says, "We are not going to do it that way anymore." Future generations will laud the course corrector.

Great is the power of connections. They draw the hunter "home from the hill" and sweeten the reunion with the prodigal. They give us a sense of safety even in unfamiliar settings. They forge friendships and create a sense of loyalty and devotion that can overcome our attachment to life itself.

An early morning visit to the cemetery can cause us to reach back, look inside, and stretch forward to strengthen the connections that bind us together and guide our sense of who we are. With proper perspective, the inevitable imperfections we see in ourselves and others are more likely to be endearing than damaging. There is a vital peace and comfort that comes in developing a sense of heritage, recognizing in oneself the traits of those who have run the race before, and feeling motivated to pass the best of them on to those who are just ready to grab the baton for their own laps around the course of life.

*We all have a longing
for belonging.*

6

Dogs in the Dark

For a number of years I jogged the roads, trails, and tracks wherever we lived. My favorite time to be out was early in the morning, preferably while it was still very dark. The dark seems to allow for a better internal focus of the senses. This time I spent, often alone, drifting along at a reasonable pace gave me an opportunity to ponder on everything from the planned events of the day to the deeper matters of the here and the hereafter.

One day at an inviting predawn hour I took advantage of the chance to jog down an isolated country road that wound through the fields surrounding the lodgings I had taken while away on a business trip. The air was crisp and clear. There was just enough moon left to cast a mild glow on the path, but plenty of dark to enfold me in the comforting cloak of the waning night.

As I padded along, feet well cushioned by thick layers of rubber and shoe foam, I was comfortable and happy. A few early birds were singing a morning song. Here and there were the scurrying sounds of a night mouse who hadn't yet called it a night. And then, way off in the distance, I could hear farm dogs barking, troubled by something unknown and probably disturbing their owners at this sleepy hour. I paid no attention and continued down the road.

The barking continued and seemed to be getting a little louder or coming closer, but it was still of no particular concern to me as I jogged along. At least not until it became obvious that the barking of these several dogs was coming toward me, ever closer and with what seemed to be a less-than-friendly tone. Suddenly the pack appeared in the distance on the road. They were headed quickly in my direction, a very unnerving sight, coupled with an ominous baying and barking that caused a rising panic in me. A pack of dogs can be vicious, and there was no place to hide, no tree to climb, nothing with which to protect myself. I was a good mile from the safe haven of my room, so outrunning the dogs was not remotely possible. There didn't seem to be a thing I could do.

But then fear gave way to anger in some seldom-needed mechanism of self-defense. Since flight was not possible, I felt a surging of the instinct to fight. I had no stick or other weapon, nothing to swing or shoot or throw. But there welled up from very deep, gathered in my throat, and burst from my mouth an exclamation somewhere between a shout and a scream. I held my ground, squared my shoulders, and yelled at the onrushing pack, "Go home!" Immediately, each of the half-dozen canines came to a halt on the pavement. They milled about for a moment in what seemed to be confusion, so I tried to clear things up for them by bellowing again, "Go home!"

Slowly the pack turned. To my amazement, they trotted back into the darkness without another sound. I supposed they were going home, so I decided to do the same. My departure (or shall we say escape) was more like a sprint than a jog. A ways down the road I was able to relax, but I couldn't help stealing a glance or two back over my shoulder.

All of us are bound to encounter some dogs in the night. Perhaps not literally, but as we move through life, it is likely that the beauty and tranquillity of the experience will be disrupted by the behavior of those who would bare their fangs at our passing. We may pose no real threat, and simply want to go quietly by, but there will be people at work, in school, or perhaps even of our own family who come at us alone or in a pack with the intention of frightening us or causing pain. Some do so out of fear of our encroachment. They have been hurt before and want to keep us and others at bay. Some may sense from us competition for their space or may want the place we occupy. Some very few people act in a way that is unreasonable and just plain mean.

When this happens, a dignified retreat is usually the best course of action. Just take a different track and leave well enough alone. When that is not possible, when they keep coming and demand a confrontation, stand your ground, square up, and, with all the power you can muster, send them back where they came from. Tell such people to "go home" and leave you alone. When they see that you are no longer afraid, that you are willing to confront their cowardly onslaught, they will likely give up the hunt and go find easier prey.

Someday they may be less aggressive, and you may be able to make peace. Until then, do not be afraid to be active. Do not miss out on the opportunities of life for fear of those who would bully you or cause you dismay.

The next morning, after the less-than-pleasant meeting with the dogs, I went jogging again. It was great.

As we stand up to them, the bullies of life will likely vanish, along with the fear they cause.

(7)

The Art of Becoming

I spoke with someone recently who had just left her teens and was entering into young adulthood. I gave her advice and tried to create some images to which she could relate, so she could develop a sense of what this new stage of her life is all about—responsibility, stability, learning, work, formalizing her preparation for life. Neither one of us thought it sounded like she was in for much fun. Thank heaven it sounds worse than it is!

As time brought our conversation to an end, I asked if she understood what I was trying to tell her. She said she did, but then posed the best question possible after such a talk: "But how do you do it?"

Excellent question! How do we implement all the good things we learn? How do we act in line with what we know? There is something in our human nature that allows us to go on doing, time and again, things we know are not right, or at least not the best for us to do. This is particularly true if our less-than-best behavior is not illegal or harmful to others and we are not, therefore, forced to change. I don't know that I could come up with detailed instructions for an easily followed, step-by-step approach to becoming who we ought to be, but perhaps a few thoughts will be helpful.

First of all, it is important to realize that the goal is to be who we are, not who we think somebody else is or who others may want us to be. The obligation we have to ourselves is to develop what is in us, who we are inside. Others may give us input in the process, but no one else can really know what and how we should be. They can know their own reaction to our behavior or make their own assessment of the correctness of what we do, but they can only surmise how well it fits with our own thoughts and feelings about who we are. We are all unique and should glory in that uniqueness.

In knowing that, though, it is also important to

realize that there is nothing wrong with some dependence and some conformity. It is perfectly normal to lean on each other for assistance. None of us is in this life alone. We all need the love and support of others. It should also be acceptable to us to corral some of our self-centered notions and align ourselves with principles of behavior that lead to the well-being of the whole group.

In becoming who we are, we should be careful not to lose our dignity in the name of individuality. We should not forget that propriety is important. Even when we know our heart is right, there is a lot to be said for acting and looking that way, too. The more we fit in with the society of which we choose to be a part, the more likely we are to be successful in the culture of that group. Little signs of behavior that might be considered rebellious, even though seemingly harmless, may allow people to take us less seriously than we hope they would.

Remember that self-development is an ongoing process, not a solitary event. It happens a little at a time, as we learn how to do it. In fact, it really lasts a lifetime. People who expect to be everything all at once are generally quite frustrated much of the time. On the other hand, those who don't expect enough of themselves fail to make much progress. They often end up wishing they had done more, tried harder, and pushed themselves further. They are frequently jealous of the accomplishments of those who did pay the price for success. The key is achieving a good balance—doing our best, but not expecting more of ourselves than is reasonable.

Another very important factor is limits. One of the most exciting things about becoming an adult is freedom from many of the limits that were imposed by parents and other care givers. The natural tendency, as soon as we get some freedom, is to resist the imposition of limitations in what we can do. That is all right to a degree, but not when it leads to excess or irresponsibility.

The most successful people set their own limits. They do not necessarily do what they do because mom and dad told them to, but because they want to do it that way. They have set their own reasonable limits and choosen to live within them. They may be more strict with themselves in some areas and less strict in others, compared to what they did at home, but the limits are theirs. They are in reality doing what they want to do. It may not be what they could do, what they are capable of doing given no limits, but they have chosen, in their pursuit of success, to limit themselves in certain areas. The interesting thing is that these kinds of limits will result in greater freedom down the road. The man who limits his spending such that he can save a little will have more money later in life and far greater financial freedom than the one who has no early limits. In fact, he will likely be making his money from the ones who spent freely early on and then have to pay it back later, with high interest.

I hesitate to use the word that best describes this limit setting, because of the bad vibrations it causes in many people, but the word is *discipline*. Discipline is the foundation of success. Disciplined eaters are thinner and generally healthier. Disciplined spenders are wealthier. Disciplined followers of religious faith are disciples indeed, and capable of loving and serving others. Those without some discipline usually wish they could be like those who have it. Again, however, balance is important. We determine the level of success we desire and then practice the level of discipline that will allow us to achieve it. And the level will vary as circumstances change in our lives. The sad thing to see is someone who keeps saying he or she will practice discipline, but who keeps putting it off in a very undisciplined manner and then winds up frustrated and disappointed with life.

Much of our sadness in life is based on wishing things were different. Undisciplined people are almost always wishing things were different. Those who have some balanced discipline in their lives may still want things to be a bit different, but, because of the limits within which they live, they see progress and maintain a lively hope that they will have what they want. Deep down, undisciplined people have a lot of hopelessness. In the back of their minds, they know they won't have what they want because they aren't doing what it takes to have it.

The last thing I would suggest is to have some

focus. Even if is quite broad and general, some direction is very important. Discipline provides momentum, but without direction we leave our destination to luck or to chance, and the odds are heavily against us arriving where we would want to be. Direction doesn't have to be unwavering. We can change direction anytime we need to. In fact, minor adjustments may be important as we gain a more clear understanding of where we want to end up.

In summary, the successful transition into adulthood would seem to be achieved through:

- appreciating and trusting our uniqueness
- accepting some dependence and conformity
- being patient with ourselves
- creating limits and disciplining ourselves
- developing a general sense of direction

Life is full of challenges, rough roads, accidents, mistakes, and surprises, but the good times far outweigh the hard times. Life is a wonderful adventure in learning, sharing, dreaming, failing, starting over, and achieving. My young friend is in for a real treat, and it will be all the more sweet for her as she incorporates the principles here mentioned. I think she'll do it. After all, she was smart enough to ask how.

In the process of becoming, the journey can also be the destination.

8

Fellow Travelers

Walking out of the store with twenty dollars in my pocket was not unusual, because I have a hard time finding anything I want that I can actually afford. It's easy to covet the expensive stuff that lies beyond the budget, but it's best to just keep walking when the temptation to purchase begins to mount beyond a reasonable person's ability to resist. Some believe maturity increases the danger of overspending. So says the adage that "the older the boys, the more expensive the toys." A plethora of credit cards has heightened the risk. On this cold morning I kept walking.

On the street outside the entrance to the mall was a man who was quite literally on the street. He sat with one leg tucked under him like a sort of pillow appendage. The other leg—well, there was no other leg, just a stump with a pinned-up pant leg. On his lap was a "will work for food" sign. What a tragic cliché.

People passed by the man without a glance. He occupied little room in their awareness. It's easy to ignore something (or someone) that quietly takes up only a small spot on the sidewalk and carefully avoids any personal contact. With his head down and his eyes lowered, all bundled in a well-worn parka and curled up on the ground, he was easy to discount and evoked little response from the more vigorous humans who quickly went about their business.

For some reason he did catch my attention. Maybe it was the contrast between the motionless lump he was and the swarm of pedestrians on the busy walk. Perhaps it was his dishevelment versus the well-kempt crowd. It might have been an unconscious comparison on my part of the deep chasm between those who have so much and those who have and seem to be so little.

I couldn't resist the desire to offer a bit of what I had saved by not buying something I didn't need anyway. Without any real contact, I dropped a ten-dollar bill into his cup and turned to move on, not wanting to draw attention to myself from him or anyone else. Before I could make my escape, however, his head came up and his eyes met mine. He smiled. His eyes were blue. He looked rather pleasant and said, "Thank you. Have a nice weekend!"

Wait a minute! That was an all-too-normal thing to say. How can we pass you by and ignore your humanity if you offer such a real-life response? What are we supposed to do if we recognize there is a personality behind the stubble on that chin? Are you somebody's husband? Is it even thinkable that a child could call you Dad or Grandpa? I guess it is! You seem like a nice enough person. Except for your circumstances, you may well be a lot like me.

"You, too," I said with a smile. And pictured him at home and hoped he would have a good weekend. I moved on with a renewed sense that all of us who live on this planet have more in common than our hurried pace allows us to realize. He was welcome to half of my twenty.

Down the street was another mendicant. He, too, attracted my attention, but unlike the first man, he was getting looks from nearly everyone. It was tough to ignore his shepherd robes and long walking staff. He stood by the crosswalk in typical head-down fashion with his hand out in a silent request for whatever monetary offering might be made. But his "I'm a little teapot" pose didn't seem to be working. All he was getting was a bit of attention. Not much money.

Oh well, the other ten in my pocket would probably do him some good. This time, however, I decided to be more interested in the person. When I placed the bill in his hand I asked, "Are you okay?"

"Yes," he replied.

Not satisfied, I inquired, "Where are you from?"

Now he raised his head. His eyes were blue also. With an interesting softness in his voice he responded, "I'm from heaven."

Taken aback, I said without thinking, "So am

I! It's nice to have you here!" My answer seemed somehow to ring true.

The begging shepherd may not have reached his conclusion about his origins in a particularly rational way. His concept of heaven may have been much different from mine. That didn't seem to matter in the brief moment in which we connected—two human beings working our way through life. Our paths were different, to be sure, but at that moment I chose not to judge or compare his way with my own. It was enough to look into his eyes, connect with a fellow traveler, share a bit of what I had to offer, and then leave him to carry on.

We owe more to those around us, much more than a few dollars. We owe them the recognition that they are worthwhile and have meaning, regardless of their situation. We owe them a friendly word and, when necessary and right, even some financial help. They live in the same world, the same country, the same city we do. Their lot in life might easily be ours except for a few changes in hard-to-predict outcomes of common choices.

I arrived back at the office without any money, but the insight I bought by offering a couple of tens to some men on the street was well worth it.

Each of us deserves to be counted in the mix that is humanity.

9

Fender Benders

Creeping along in rush-hour traffic, the only stimulation I could find was public radio and the anticipation of a warm dinner. The stress and anxiety of the workday were just beginning to dissipate, but the traffic wasn't helping much. I could have made it through the intersection on the next green light if the guy in front of me would have moved a little faster and narrowed the gap between him and the car ahead of him. The lady in the car behind me was not a bit shy about keeping on my bumper. I glanced in the rearview mirror, hoping she was paying attention. The light turned yellow and one more car sneaked through, but not Mr. Conservative in front of me. Just then, my head jerked back as Mrs. Tailgater finally got her wish—to put her bumper where my bumper was supposed to be.

Not much of a crash, but I thought I'd better take a look.

Out of the car, on foot in the crowded street, I felt all eyes on me as I surveyed the damage. I couldn't see even a scratch. She rolled down the window, and I told her there was no damage. She offered no apology, just a lame excuse about it being a new car and she wasn't used to the length. I resisted making the suggestion that discretion is the better part of valor; just stay back a little and you won't be hitting the people ahead of you. Instead, I wished her well and climbed back into my car. By now they had cleared out ahead of me and I could move right up to the light. Next time through would be my turn. Mine and Mrs. Tailgater's. Luckily, she went straight as I turned onto a cross street and headed for home.

Even as home came closer, I couldn't help but think of Mrs. Tailgater. What was she thinking? If she couldn't judge the length of her car, why didn't she keep her distance? Was she stupid? Was she mean? Did she plan to hit my car?

Of course not.

She was just a regular person, trying to get home safely. Her mind somewhat numbed by the fatigue of a workday and the snail pace of the traffic, her attention had waned for a moment and she had allowed her car to creep forward an inch too far. No real harm done. No reason for me to be angry or to harshly judge her competence.

None of us is free from the occasional bumps and scrapes of human interaction. We all receive a few here and there, and we probably give as many as we get. None of those who offend are part of a great conspiracy to do us harm, nor are we acting with malice toward any of our neighbors. Fender benders are a natural hazard of life, just a part of getting around in the world.

One of the best experiences I have had with another person came after one of these rough encounters. He didn't know me, and I didn't know him. I'm sure he was actually unaware that I was a bit banged up by his behavior.

We were sitting in a large public eating area, he and his friends at one table and I alone at another. I had never seen him before. He was talking so loudly that I honestly couldn't help but overhear the harsh criticism he was leveling at some folks I did know. He was really venting his frustration, but from what he was saying, I could tell he didn't really know what he was talking about. That made his remarks all the more bothersome, and I was sorely tempted to confront him on the spot and correct and condemn what was clearly wrong and seemed to be mean and ugly talk. As it was, I just walked away.

As I thought about the experience, however, it felt all the more important to set him straight and let him know the facts in the matter about which he was so angry. So, the next time I saw him in the area, I asked a friend who this guy was. I was able to learn his name and where he worked, so later I called him on the telephone, introduced myself, and asked him to come to my office for a chat. He was willing to come, like a lamb to the slaughter. But then there came to my mind memories of times I had spoken without clear understanding. By the time he arrived, my attitude was changed. My great hope was simply to listen to his feelings, to try to understand and maybe even help, and, most of all, to make a new friend.

He remembered well the conversation in which he had fumed with his friends over lunch. When I told him I had some interest in the matter he was discussing, and wondered if he would mind sharing his feelings with me, he became very apologetic and quickly confessed that he was wrong to have spoken out as he did. He turned out to be a great guy and one upon whom our office could call for future help. I made a new friend, and I hope he did too.

As we steer about in the bumper-car ride of life, we cannot avoid every collision. Some are purely accidental, some may be a bit calculated, but most fender benders are the result of simple human frailty and miscalculation. Every day of this life is new to us, and we may have a hard time getting used to the thing. I may bump into you, you'll probably bump into me a time or two, but hopefully no one will be hurt and we can just learn from the experience. Maybe we can even make a new friend in the process.

Most offense is unintentional.
If we really knew the offender,
he or she would likely
be a friend.

(10)

The Genuine Article

More than a thousand people were gathered in the large hall. The program was billed as marriage enrichment, and they had all come together to learn what they could about being better husbands and wives. There were young couples looking hopeful and rapidly taking notes. Some of them appeared to realize that the honeymoon was over and it was time to learn how to make this thing really work. There were senior couples looking self-satisfied, kind of parading their success-by-longevity relationships. And there were a few of those about to embark upon the sometimes stormy seas of matrimony. They looked . . . well, they looked around mostly, sizing up their fellow conferencegoers and wondering how they would fare in this marriage business. Most of these latter couples gave each other fawning glances, but a few looked like they were there to gather ammunition for a crusade to corral the infidel to whom they would soon be joined in solemn covenant. More than five hundred couples were there, hoping for some insight to guide them along.

The speakers weren't bad. Some were better prepared than others. One or two had something meaningful to say. There was plenty of encouragement and "hang in there" advice. So far we hadn't learned a lot, but we were feeling pretty good. Then the keynote speaker was introduced.

Our final extoller of the glories of marriage was a frail little lady of nearly ninety years of age. As she worked her way to the podium, the whole group sat forward a little, offering their support to her somewhat shaky steps. She entered the spotlight, focused on the microphone, and grimaced as she was blinded by the artificial brightness. Her white hair, illuminated by the light, surrounded her head like a halo. She wore a smile that offered all the more proof of her angelic status, and there was a twinkle in her eye that convinced us she had something to say.

Indeed she did have something to tell the group. She spoke of over sixty years of marriage, of the joys and tears, of the hopes and fears that made the journey with her husband such an adventure. She spoke of his foibles, and he smiled and squirmed a bit in his seat behind her, but you could tell he was very proud of his partner and companion, the mother of his children, as she counseled and taught the audience of enthralled listeners.

Hers was a story of many years of perseverance in the bearing of five children and in providing a stable and positive home in which they could thrive and prepare for their own flight from the family nest. Without falling victim to the pitfalls of pretense or self-deprecation, she spoke of her own development as a woman and expressed gratitude for the freedom to grow that had been sincerely encouraged by her good mate. As an able spokesperson for the institution, she helped us all to understand better that building a good marriage isn't easy, but it can be more than worth it.

As she finished, there was a quiet second or two as her message of hard work, nurturing, and love sank into the hearts of the participants. Then the place erupted into a roar of applause with the crowd standing in honor of the speaker. Her honest, optimistic manner had won the day and offered all the opportunity to share in a determination to make their own marriages stronger.

After the meeting, several of us shared our feelings about the experience. Most of the talk centered on our final speaker. Much praise was offered, but I think the best thing said about her came from one man who commented, "She's the genuine article."

In a world where so much is artificial and so many are only superficially living their lives, it is awesome to meet up with people who have managed to walk through the minefield of everyday experience without tripping a wire and demolishing their originality, refitting their torn existence with the prosthetics of affectation and charade. It is a rare person, indeed, who has learned to like who he or she really is and to become very good at actually being that person.

Adjustment to life circumstances is essential, of course. I think our matriarchal speaker had made many compromises as she responded to those around her. But being real isn't just doing your own thing; it's not a matter of selfishness. In fact, selfish people are denying a huge part of what is real in their lives. Other people are real. They have actual needs and realistic desires. Sometimes, by assisting others to bring their own hopes into fruition, we come a lot closer to realizing our own unique destiny. Many people are so caught up in self-development that they don't have time simply to be who they already are. Somebody once said something about finding more of yourself the more you give yourself away.

So, there she had stood, a wonderful woman who had given so much and become even more. She considered herself no better than anyone else, but realized she was no worse. A good person, doing her best, loving those around her, intent on reaching her potential—but not at the expense of serving others—she neither praised herself nor apologized for living. She was truly the genuine article.

When you give yourself away in service to others, you will find real meaning in life and create the ultimate you.

Just Hold Me

One of the great western dramas is a wonderful film entitled *Shane,* starring Alan Ladd as a handsome, charming gunfighter with hopes of finding a life without violence. This was not an easy task in the Wild West of Hollywood's creation. The results are quite predictable, but it makes for a good movie, anyway.

Running almost unnoticed in the story is an interesting subplot regarding Shane and the wife of the homesteader for whom he is working. Shane seems to be a source of some fascination for the woman, who has very little excitement in her life of toil and hardship. Her down-to-earth and faithful character is somewhat compromised for a time as she allows her feelings to wander and develops a little crush on the alluring stranger.

In one scene, she and Shane are alone in the main room of the cabin. Her husband and son have gone off to prepare for bed. She stands close to Shane, who is seated at the table, and they share a tender moment. Just then the boy calls, and the woman leaves the room with the expectation of a quick return. When she comes back, Shane has left. The distracted farmer's wife stands gazing dreamily out the doorway after this intriguing man. Quickly the door of the bedroom opens, and the homesteader sees his wife looking at their retreating guest. Somewhat naively, the farmer says to his wife, "What's the matter, honey?" The good woman turns and almost runs back to reality and the solid safety to be found in the arms of her noble husband. "Hold me," she implores. "Don't say anything, just hold me—tight."

It is easy in the often routine and occasionally dull exercise of everyday life to long for something more exciting and stimulating. Every now and then a person, place, or thing crops up that looks more appealing than that with which we are so familiar. Submerged hopes and desires bubble to the surface, and feelings of longing may tug at our hearts. The sports car we have always wanted, the six-figure income that has eluded us, or perhaps even a person other than our spouse who seems to fit the dream mold we created in our youthful minds— any of these, and many other things, can sing a siren song that lifts us into the netherworld of fantasy. The escape from the mundane reality of regular existence can seem spellbinding.

There is nothing inherently wrong with hopes and dreams and wishes. They should be pursued to their reasonable ends. But there comes a time in our reverie when it may be vital to turn and almost run to the arms of someone or something real that will bring us back to the ground.

It can be very dangerous to follow our fantasies down a path of thoughtless quest, ignoring the possible consequences of our behavior. We can inflict much trauma on ourselves and upon those who see our folly. Their often frantic efforts to open our eyes before the rude awakening jerks us back to our senses can be painful. Sadly, sometimes the damage is so complete that return to former safe havens is rendered impossible.

I recall working with a man who was nearly suicidal because of ongoing serious money problems. He was not a bad fellow, but he was understandably failing to make a living selling summer services in snowy January. We talked about his financial situation, and I asked what kind of car he drove. "Oh," he said with pride, "I drive a beautiful new (such-and-such). It's just the car I've always wanted." It turned out that he was going in the hole each month almost exactly the amount of the payment on his dream car. Meanwhile, his children had a dysfunctional dad and his wife was forced to fend off the bill collectors. He needed grounding.

All too common are the tragic circumstances of good family men and women who tire of the run-of-the-mill, often unheralded work of bringing home the bacon and raising the youngsters who eat it. Like the homesteader's wife in *Shane,* they gaze longingly after what appears to be the retreating possibility for a truly happy life. Then comes the destroyer disguised as the wonderful opportunity they have been waiting for. The chance of a lifetime in a risky business proposition. An investment that's sure to pay off in a big way. Or, perhaps most dangerous of all, a friend of the opposite gender in whom they can really confide—finally, someone who understands their deepest feelings.

Unwilling to listen to reason or even to the pleadings of anxious loved ones, feet wafting just above the ground, they drift in fantastic bliss, thinking only of their need to finally achieve that well-deserved measure of happiness. At such a time, they can be so duped by selfish desire that it is nearly impossible for them to foresee the consequences of their headlong pursuit of what they think they want. Financial ruin is a frequent result. Or what was once a potentially happy family can quickly become a disillusioned former companion and brokenhearted children.

It is wonderful to see people who have a dream and go for it with passion, confidence, and unwavering determination. Tremendous personal growth and meaningful contribution can be realized by those who are willing to give the extra effort or walk the narrow path that is dictated by their dreams. But the most successful of these also realize that they may be limited by vows and restrained by responsibilities that are not subject to honest abandonment.

One of the great revelations of my life was the powerful realization that I would rarely go wrong if I just listened to my wife. She has been the great grounding influence in my life. We might also turn for guidance to some other trusted person, to the sacred or secular writings of inspiring authors, or simply to a quiet hour of meditative self-appraisal. Each of these can provide an immovable, fixed point by which we can navigate. If we do so, certain opportunities may have to be foregone, but we will probably never feel any lasting remorse for the decisions we make.

In the end, Shane rode off into the sunset (actually the sunrise), and the farmer's wife remained with her devoted companion. She may have wondered wistfully what life would have been like with the man in buckskin, but I believe that when she heard the happy footsteps of her children and shared a moment with her husband surveying the land they had worked so hard to tame, she was brought back to earth and felt the great joy of a wholesome normalcy. What a gift is grounding.

It is all right to have your head in the clouds, as long as your feet are firmly on the ground.

(12)

The Verbal Knockout

When the televised boxing match began, my wife left the room. Too violent for her. All the kids but one drifted away to something more meaningful. Only our youngest daughter was interested in watching the mayhem with her father, so we sat in the semidarkness enthralled by the spectacle of fisticuffs. There was something very basic, even visceral, about the sweat, the blood, the swollen eyes and flat noses of the fighters. A man in blue trunks and one in white, like desperate predators in opposite corners of the cage, ready to pounce again as soon as they gained their breath.

We watched several rounds of jabbing and sparring until blue trunks saw an opening and landed a heavy blow to the head of his opponent. White trunks reeled and tried to protect himself.

Another blow to the head and then one to the mid-section and another to the head. He was dazed and hurt. With no hope for the mercy of a saving bell, the injured white trunks fell onto his attacker, embracing him in a fearsome clench.

"Why doesn't he run away?" asked my little girl. "Why doesn't he back up so the other guy can't hit him?"

Good questions. It looked like getting close to the powerful fists of blue trunks was the last thing the man in white ought to be doing. The square ring offers few hiding places, but it seemed to my daughter that he would be wiser to get on his boxing bicycle and try to outrun the pummeling. Not so. Retreating when hurt usually allows the opponent to step up and throw another blow, sometimes a knockout.

When a boxer gets tired or hurt, often the best thing he can do is get in close and hang on to the other fighter. When he moves in to the point of embracing his opponent in a sort of sweaty bear hug, he just can't be hit. The aggressor has lost his leverage, and the pair are too close to allow either one to get a good swing. Not a bad strategy, even for those of us who have no pugilistic ambitions.

When someone lands a verbal punch, the natural reaction is to back up or run. It hurts when we get socked with a stiff jab from a sharp tongue. But, just as with an unskilled boxer, backing off can easily set us up for a more severe beating. It's usually best to move in and neutralize our opponent's ability to strike.

On more than one occasion, an individual has lashed out at me for some perceived wrong I have committed. Once or twice I have responded with a verbal comeback that did nothing but excite my opponent to throw some more my way. Sometimes I have figuratively run away or at least backed off, allowing the one who saw me as the enemy to have even more room to fight. The far better strategy has been to move in close.

Hey, you really seem angry. Slow down, talk about it, what went wrong.

Some huffing and puffing, an explanation of my supposed error, but no more punches thrown.

You're kidding. I had no idea. I'm really sorry you saw it that way.

The fight is over. A little more explanation. An increase in understanding. If you're lucky, some real communication and a strengthening of the relationship. None of that would have been likely if you had backed up or run away.

Slip his punches. Step into him. Minimize his advantage. Keep him off balance. Don't let him swing. Good advice for a dazed boxer. Perhaps even better for a fighter in a war of words.

Embrace your opponent in a way that lessens the threat and leads to understanding.

(13)

Cows in the Corn

There is hardly anything better to eat than fresh garden vegetables. You don't pick them until they're ripe and ready to be tasted. Then, the quicker they go from garden to dinner table, the better. It's only natural that a few don't even make it to the table, but are savored right from the pod, stalk, or stem. Delicious.

I couldn't believe my good fortune when our neighbor Tom asked us to share with his family their sizeable garden plot. Tom was raised making plants grow and taught biology and horticulture at the local high school. He really knew how to get the most out of a tomato vine and a corn stalk.

Speaking of corn, that was one of Tom's specialties. He knew which variety could reach its potential in the local soil. He knew just when to plant it and how to care for it so the corn would be sweet. I could taste it already.

Tom had a small farm located about a mile from our home. It was mostly a hobby for him, but he had some cows, a few pigs, and a large garden plot consisting of about twelve rows nearly a hundred feet long. That's a lot of garden! It didn't take me long to understand why Tom was so willing to bring us in on the operation. The agreement was that he would supply the land, the tools, the seed, and the fertilizer (actually the cows offered most of that), and I would take charge of most of the weeding and a good deal of the irrigation. Keeping that much garden free of weeds and well watered is not easy. It takes a lot of time.

Nearly every Saturday morning during the growing season I was in the garden, hoe in hand, working up blisters on my city-slicker palms. I loved it and did a pretty good job, except for the time I rooted up Tom's prize peppers. Hey, they looked like weeds to me!

It was so great to watch the plants grow, nurse them along, and anticipate the harvest. Ah, the harvest. We had peas, tomatoes, potatoes, squash of several varieties, pumpkins, peppers (hot, medium, and cold), and corn. Six rows of sweet corn, rising right up to the elephant's eye and creating visions in our heads of bright yellow ears, hot, succulent, and dripping with butter.

The dream of such eating pleasure made all the weeding well worth it. Even when I was hoeing in the heat with the mosquitoes buzzing and biting, sweat stinging my eyes and corn-pollen allergies threatening to clog every opening for my very breath, it was worth it. The corn would make all the work worth it.

Late one Friday evening, Tom stopped by with the good news. "The corn is ready," he declared, "and it's wonderful." Great! We really had a good crop. I planned to pick enough the next morning to allow for a sweet corn overdose by all interested parties. I had worked for it. We would enjoy it.

As the sun rose on Saturday morning, I had no desire to stay in bed. On with my work boots and off to the farm. I could almost hear the corn calling.

As I drove up to the garden plot, my heart raced with almost gluttonous anticipation. But wait. Just a minute. What on earth . . . where was the corn? It was gone. All six rows had disappeared.

I raced from the car to the scene of the crime. And a crime it was. Long rows of beautiful sweet corn, the object of my toil, the subject of my epicurean lust, all gone. Only a few shredded stalks remained and here an ear and there an ear, trampled into the ground.

Tom's cows had gotten out in the night, and the whole herd had headed directly for the corn patch. It seems corn stalks and the fresh ears they carry are like candy to a cow. They had beaten us to the feast and left nothing in their tracks but tracks.

What a waste and a terrible disappointment! I picked up an overripe tomato and threw it in the direction of the cow corral, now safely holding its charges. *Rotten cows,* I whispered through clenched teeth. One of them looked my way, calmly chewing her cud. *Probably chewing on sweet corn,* I mumbled. I kicked a pumpkin and slapped at a pea vine in total frustration. And then I began to laugh.

I laughed all the way home. The whole family laughed as we pictured the herd in their midnight raid of our corn patch. We figured they must have overheard Tom say the time was right for picking and then plotted their escape from the corral. How hilarious that we should work so hard and then, just before our culinary triumph, have the cows steal it all like bovine burglars. Well, I hoped they enjoyed it. We bought a few ears from the local grocer and enjoyed some good corn anyway.

At the end of the season, Tom and I plowed under the remains of the vegetation and prepared the ground for the next year. We chuckled a bit over the loss of the sweet corn, but remembered fondly the other wonderful fruits of this special garden plot, all to be enjoyed again next year.

I looked forward to another planting, to another season of irrigating, weeding, and longing for fresh-tasting produce. I realized that working in the soil really does renew a person's soul. Dirt beneath the fingernails is somehow cleansing. A few callouses on the palms of your hands will ward off hopelessness and teach the powerful lessons associated with the law of the harvest.

It didn't matter that we had no corn. The lasting joy of this garden, and of most worthwhile work, was not in the having, but in the doing.

The process of acquiring something is often more satisfying than actually owning it.

(14)

Can You Imagine?

Is it a rocket ship or just a box that used to hold something far more earthbound? Could that be a time machine or simply a large cardboard container? It all depends on your perspective and whether or not you've retained the ability you had as a child to look past the stark reality of an object, to see in your imagination what it might become . . . and what you might become with it.

To imagine is to overcome the laws of physics, to set aside the limitations of biology and environment, and to allow the mind to soar into the ethereal realms of boundless possibility. What awaits you there is completely up to you.

I was reminded of this recently when my little granddaughter received a holiday gift. It was a delightful present and one that will give her many hours of pleasure. But no amount of fun derived from this toy will exceed that which she seemed to receive by playing with the paper in which it was wrapped. Heaven knows where she went with it in her imagination, but she certainly seemed to have a wonderful time as she tossed it, wore it like a wrap and then like a hat, used it to shield out the world, and occasionally peered mysteriously from behind it. What a special plaything it became, as the colorful wrapping paper turned into anything she wanted it to be. Watching her, I saw it transformed from a many-colored cloak to a nomad's headdress to a mystical oriental screen. The look on her face told the careful observer that exotic tales might be spun in her mind as the magical paper carried her about like Aladdin's enchanted carpet. I hope she can hold on to the ability to ride that marvelous rug of possibilities.

Reading helps maintain the place of imagination beyond early childhood. With great fondness, I recall the hours I spent as a young boy swinging through the heights of the jungle with friends Tarzan and his son, exploring the depths of the

Great Barrier Reef with a couple of adventurous fictional boys, spending a hard winter in a rabbit den, and understanding Ben Franklin from the viewpoint of a church mouse.

As adults, many of us have climbed the highest mountains, sailed the briny deep, and skulked through the shadows of the Cold War guided by the writing of favorite novelists and stimulated by the smoldering remnants of imagination left over from the fires of youthful whimsy. Like any sweet, too much nonnutritional literary fantasizing can leave us underfed, but a little is mighty tasty.

Perhaps we lose too early our ability to travel the road of imagination. We become caught up in the demands of life, which force us to focus on the here and now, the concrete facts of our material existence. We are faced with stiff competition in almost constant efforts to come off victorious in a race with the clock, with fellow workers, with "the Joneses," even with the natural process of aging. *Better face reality, kid, life is tough. You're swimming with sharks out there. The guy in the next office, the junk food you love to eat, and gravity itself are all out to get you in the end. If you let down for just a moment, they'll eat you alive!* There is a lot of imagination in such a warning, but somehow it gets lost in the fear spawned by that kind of advice.

Each one of us is unique in the way we deal with the world around us. Some of us prefer to spend the majority of our time with other people, while some would rather work on a machine that doesn't talk back. A good share of us make our decisions based on an emotional response. Others are far more logical in their consideration and leave feelings out of the process.

There are those of us who base our appraisal of life almost exclusively on reason and the somewhat rigid analysis of what we can see, hear, touch, smell, and taste. If a matter doesn't fit into our basic means of sensory discernment, we have a hard time giving it much attention. For those who prefer the imaginative over the sensing side of the equation, the possibilities matter even more than the realities, and intuition plays a more prominent role in life than mere facts. These individuals are less prone to be inhibited by the limits that appear to be imposed by self, setting, or science.

It is in balance that we realize the most and the best in matters of perception. The greatest results seem to come from a good mix of each way of deciding what is. Grounded in facts, the use of imagination has allowed for the development of such wonders as the electric light and the computer chip. Imagination can lead us to the bottom of a deep ocean canyon with Seussian fishes or into the airlessness of space where, quite literally, up and down do not exist.

In all of our acquiring, let's spend a little time trying not to lose that which we have had since our toddling days, that with which we seem to have come naturally into the world—our imagination. Dally a bit, and do not feel guilty about reading something that takes you, in your mind, someplace you're not otherwise likely to go. Play with the wrapping paper. Toy with the cardboard box. Renew and remake yourself into whatever you would like, wherever you wish, and for as long as you need. The wonder of reality will only be enhanced by the creative force of your imagining, and the unique, childlike you will shine a little brighter, like it used to.

A little imagining can expand the truth and give new life to the power of our senses.

(15)

Leslie of Liverpool

He looked a little pitiful sitting by himself at the end of the long corridor. A rather small Englishman with thin and scruffy hair, not the kind to make a first-glance good impression. Somehow, images of the comic actor Stan Laurel came to mind when I first saw Leslie.

Leslie was a security guard in a building in Chorley, England, a building that had a few too many security guards. I'm not sure what they expected would render the place insecure, but whatever it was, they were certainly prepared. The guards were placed with a strategy designed, I suppose, to fend off whatever evil might lurk in the hearts of calculating men. And Leslie must have been assigned his post as an integral part of some grand defensive tactic.

In fact, Leslie was guarding a locked door at the end of a little-used hallway. Why, I cannot say. No bare-handed human could get through the heavy, bolted door. Whatever could break it down, should someone for some unknown reason want to break it down, would not be deterred by diminutive Leslie. The main threat from this direction was not likely to be from any outside source of danger, but from the almost deadly boredom that filled the air at the end of the hall such that I didn't know how Leslie could breathe.

I couldn't help but feel sorry for this poor man. I introduced myself, hoping a moment of conversation might ease the monotony some.

"And your name?" I asked.

"Leslie," he said quietly, perhaps a little annoyed at my intrusion.

"And where are you from, Leslie?"

"Liverpool."

"Ah," I quipped, "Leslie of Liverpool."

He grinned a bit sheepishly and probably thought I was making fun of him. Maybe I was.

Leslie was very pleasant, though, and quickly

my impression of the foolish actor was completely dispelled. Here was a bright, middle-aged man with a family to care for. He wasn't a big man, but not quite as small as I had first thought.

I soon learned that Leslie was a volunteer. Yes, he worked as a security guard in another city, in Liverpool actually, but this post was manned as a favor to a friend and he wasn't getting a dime for being there.

"Leslie," I said, "could I get you a softer chair?"

"No," said he, "this one will do."

"Well," I proposed, "do you really need to be here? Nothing seems likely to happen."

He looked around as if to quickly assess the current level of security.

"I'll just do what I've been asked," he said in his thick Liverpudlian accent. "I'll just do me duty."

"May I at least bring you a can of juice or something? You could man your post and still drink some juice."

"No, thanks," he replied with a certain firmness in his voice, "I'll just do me duty."

I finally gave up. "Okay, have a good evening," I said in parting. I admit I was not very sympathetic to Leslie's sense of duty. It seemed a bit overzealous to me.

That night I had an interesting dream. I was in England, so it is not surprising that it was a dream of knights and heavy armor and white chargers. There were brave fighting scenes and charging hordes and clanging swords.

One knight stood out among all the rest. I don't remember if his armor was actually shining, but he was strong and true and the hero of my dream.

As the hero-knight emerged victorious, he stopped and dismounted his powerful steed. He stood before me, removed his helmet with dignity, and quietly introduced himself.

"Good day, sir," he said calmly. "I am Leslie, Leslie of Liverpool."

I awoke with a start. Wide awake. And I saw clearly the courage of Leslie.

He had been asked to perform a rather per-functory task, but his sense of honor and duty caused him to do it to the very best of his ability. I think he would have guarded the Royal Jewels with no more pride or careful attention. Even as a volunteer, not being paid at all and sitting alone in that empty hall, he felt a commitment to muster all his professional skill and to focus on the perform-ance of his duty. Even with distractors and detrac-tors like me around, he was determined to stay on track and do it right.

Leslie taught me that to do your duty is to set aside self and give heart and mind to the higher good. It's the Leslies of the world, each one doing her or his duty, that allow us all to rise above our natural human meanness and achieve what none could do alone. To give it your all, even when the individual task seems truly menial, that is the ful-fillment of duty.

The next evening as I was leaving the building I looked in hope for Leslie. He was there again, at the end of the hall, a knight in invisible armor doing his duty. I was glad to see him. We greeted each other. I didn't tell him why, but I asked a passerby to take my picture standing next to Leslie. I wanted to remember what a hero looks like and to prove that I had known one.

I'll just do me duty. That's the stuff of real power. Lancelot, Gawain, and Galahad are legendary for cunning and strength, but Leslie of Liverpool, the great doer of duty, is my hero.

I'll just do me duty.

Letting Go

Junior high school was an exciting time in my young life. The discovery of academics, girls, and sports made for a great combination. There was always something to do! Admittedly, my favorite classes were physical education and lunch, but I also learned to read for more than just pure entertainment. Reading for the purpose of learning was like turning on a light, and it brought with it a greater vision of the real purpose of education.

The girl stuff remained a mysterious yet powerful influence lurking in the shadows of my early teen existence. It occasionally burst forth to set the world aglow for a week or two, until either she or I lost interest. Just long enough to accumulate a few love notes and her name written boldly on my looseleaf, and then back into the shadows it crept.

No harm done, and I could still hit the ball just as far.

In ninth grade, the coaches built into our sports education an introduction to gymnastics: forward rolls, backward extensions, and even a handspring or two. We bruised our armpits on the parallel bars and grew a few blisters swinging on the high bar. It was great fun, but every now and then a bit scary.

One day, the coaches decided to see who would really go for it on the high bar. All the students and a few coaches crowded around the bar and the floor-softening mats. One boy began swinging back and forth, higher and higher to build his momentum, with the idea in mind of letting go at just the right moment on the upswing and rolling in the air in a flip before landing on the mat—hopefully, feet first. Few had the courage to even attempt such a death-defying feat.

When the coach looked my way and motioned for me to grab the bar and start swinging, I eagerly jumped to the task. A little spit, a cloud of chalk dust on my hands, and up to the bar I leapt. Now swinging, now gaining some speed and height, it was time to attempt a flip off the bar.

To my surprise, I couldn't let go. The more I determined to cast my body to the wind, to challenge the forces of gravity, to avoid the humiliation of failure, the tighter became my grasp on that cold steel bar.

"Let go," cried the coach. "Now!" he yelled.

"You can do it!" screamed my classmates in futile support. But the more they coaxed, the firmer my grip became.

Finally, dropping to the ground in defeat, I looked up at that bar and pronounced it a demon. Of course, I couldn't let go. I wanted to. I wasn't afraid, but it had me in its evil clutches. It conquered us all that day. Not a boy who tried was able to wrest himself free of the monster bar. Not one of us soared. Not a flip was performed. It beat every one of us.

I doubt that any of us in that class ever became accomplished gymnasts, and that's not a particularly bad thing. Such athletic feats are not for everybody and are certainly not the ultimate mark of success. But one thing is certain: Each of us had to learn, at one time or another, how to let go of the personal demon, whatever it might be, that tightened our grip on security and prevented our reaching the heights.

For the shy boy, the one who rarely said a word, it was overcoming his fear of speaking out. He had to let go of the ghost of silence and learn to express deeply held thoughts. The one who seemed to lack intellectual skill had to struggle from the clasp of morbid inadequacy and find his place to excel. The kid who saw himself as being ugly, and often felt scorned by his peers, had to leap from the devil-made bar of self-loathing and, forgetting himself, reach out to help others.

In the end, that steel bar in the gym class was nothing in comparison to the other letting go that had to be done. The relief of finally dropping off the high bar and walking away from the potentially bone-crushing landing was a passing thing for a junior high boy. But none of us could finally avoid the time—maybe several times in our lives— when we would have to overcome the imp of fear, jump from our hiding place, and fly into the world of achievement.

Such is life, even the very purpose of life, to trust in ourselves and all we hold sacred, to learn to let go of the bar.

The view from the heights is reserved for those who are willing to set themselves free.

(17)

Scruffy

Our family of five small children with big appetites didn't ever send to the garbage very much that was edible. If the bowl was not emptied at dinnertime, whatever had graced our table became a tantalizing leftover to be eagerly consumed as a microwave special by whichever lucky child arrived home first the next day. So I was quite surprised when I found our garbage can had been raided by a roving scrap bandit.

I quizzed the kids to see if they could identify our thief-in-the-night. No one could, but my son told of seeing a mysterious, doglike ball of fur skulking through the backyard just a few days before. A likely suspect.

The next morning, when the garbage had once again been raided, we decided to try to prevent the ransacking of the refuse can by putting a little something where the obviously hungry mutt could get to it without making a mess. After a few days of this we finally spied him—the mangiest, filthiest little mongrel I had ever seen. His light-colored coat was snarled and matted, and he was gnawing on some doggy delicacy with an air of skittishness that spoke of his having been chased away from his meal by more than one irate homeowner.

This small dog presented such a pitiful sight that my rescue reflex was immediately piqued. As I approached him to test his friendliness, I expected him to run off, but all he did was cower down and whimper. He didn't move when I scratched his head. I figured he was just too weak to try to escape. Up close he appeared even dirtier and in worse shape than we had thought. He was the scruffiest thing we had ever seen. Scruffy! The perfect moniker for our nameless dinner guest.

We decided to clean Scruffy up and give him a decent meal. A plastic tub accommodated his size quite well as we doused him with a bucket of water, held him tight to trickle shampoo over his snarly coat, and massaged the suds into cleansing lather. The rinse water was gray with weeks' or even months' worth of accumulated grime. Scruffy seemed to enjoy it as we poured on bucket after bucket and then shampooed again, just to be sure he was as clean as we could get him. After the final rinsing, he showed his gratitude with a flurry of shakes that sent a drenching shower into the faces of all of his would-be groomers. At least the water was clean.

From that moment on, Scruffy was a different animal. He ceased his cowering and began a tongue-enhanced pant that seemed to reveal a happy smile behind the fur that covered his face. After eating the food we set before him, he ran around the yard jumping and barking in a display of pure joy and excitement. Every so often he stopped at the feet of whoever was near and waited for a pat or a rub or a scratch; then he was off again running in circles, up the yard and back again, until it was time for another love pat by one of us who shared his revelry.

Scruffy stayed around for several days. We fed

him and gave him a soft rug to sleep on and laughed at his clowning in the yard. One morning we found a few moldy tortillas on the front step. Scruffy was returning our kindness at the expense of some neighbor's garbage! The real personality in that little dog was so fun and lovable, far different from what we had supposed when first he came into our lives.

One day we missed the canine vagabond of whom we had grown so fond. I suppose his wanderlust got the better of him, and he went in search of more friends and easy pickings from someone else's garbage can. We have never forgotten him, though, and the incredible transformation that came about through the showing of a bit of kindness.

We can see the same miraculous change in people. I spied an old man, head down and shuffling, walking slowly toward me on the sidewalk. He had a few days' growth of beard and was unkempt in his dress. He looked like a man who had left behind the happy days of his life and lived now in sweet memory but lonely and bitter reality.

As the scruffy man approached, I blurted out a cheery, "Good morning, sir!" To my surprise and true delight, he lifted his head and, with a grin as wide as a well-fed puppy, responded, "Good morning to you!" The lonely old man before my eyes vanished in an instant, and the lovable side of his nature came out when just a little kindness was sent his way.

I think they call it nurturing, that offering of self to those around us who need some loving and lifting. And it's not just the stray dog and the lonely widower who deserve such attention. Perhaps even more in want are those around us whose existence and well-being we take so very much for granted. Our wives or husbands, moms or dads or kids are just as much in need of an overt demonstration of our love, some identifiable kindness that they will notice and that will bring joy and maybe even a silly grin into their lives. People soften and warm to a little nurturing. It will help them now, and they'll remember it later. The recollection of such simple acts may see them through a dark hour down the road when we're not there in person.

Those around us need to know we share their pain and are willing to bear a portion of whatever burden they may carry, not just when it's convenient or uncomplicated, but whenever the need exists. If a man's wife or one of his children has a problem, so does he. There should be no mistake. We are not in this alone, and our responsibility to love is as great as our right to be loved. A little considerate effort from us can turn the night to day for one who longs for such a kindly touch.

There is a miracle formula in which a very small addition of love creates an overflowing reaction of happiness. The person who mixes the generous potion and the thirsty one who drinks from the gracious cup are both better for the experience. Much will be received even when only a little is lovingly given.

Our right to be cared for is exceeded only by our duty to nurture others.

No Way Out

My wife has a great love for art and architecture. She has taught me to look at buildings from the perspective of the artist as well as the engineer. I am neither, but I have come to realize that there are two roles a structure can play in our lives. She says it has to do with form and function. I refer to it as what the building is, compared to what the building does. The additional insight has added immensely to my appreciation for all that goes into the fabrication of a beautiful and a useful edifice.

We visited an art museum and marveled at the lines of the building itself in addition to the incredible masterworks contained therein. Though the museum structure could be seen by some as not much more than a warehouse for art, the wonderful works of the artists were made all the more impressive by the physical facility in which they were placed. Each was well-served by the other and made our experience more complete.

In another exceptional building, we saw a feature designed by the architect for no obvious function, but which provoked in us a powerful response. In the most ornate room, the creator of this structure had placed beautiful door frames on the walls. They matched the frames located in other parts of the building, but these were of particular interest because they contained no doors. There was no door handle for opening and closing, no hinge upon which the door might swing, in fact, no opening at all, just a lovely frame. One might easily have approached the frame looking for an exit or entrance, but such would be sought in vain. No way in and no way out through these pretend portals.

The image of doors without knobs brings to mind the circumstance in which so many have found themselves. It is not uncommon for people to reach a point in life where they feel that the only doors available to them are closed and provide no means of escape. They feel trapped, unable to move forward or go back. No solutions seem to be available, and few options present themselves.

I was literally in that position on one memorable occasion. I was staying by myself in an old hotel. It was so old that the rooms did not have private baths, but there was only one between two rooms. The bathroom doors did have knobs, but the locking system was ancient. In order to lock the door, one simply turned a small piece built into the doorknob. The locking piece was, however, on the bedroom side of the door, not on the bathroom side. That way the stranger next door could use the bathroom, but I could lock the door so he would not have access to my room.

Interestingly, when the door was opened from the bedroom side, the lock did not automatically disengage, as you might expect. If you weren't careful, you could turn the knob, open the door, go into the bathroom, and close it again, and if you didn't turn the little locking piece, the door would remain locked. You could find yourself locked in the bathroom with no easy way out.

I awakened early in the morning, groggily shed my clothing, grabbed a bar of soap, and stepped sleepily into the bathroom. As the door latched, I was shocked awake with the realization that I had failed to turn the locking piece, which was now located on the wrong side of a locked door. Oops. I was locked out of my own room, and in a state that did not easily lend itself to interaction with others. Well, I would just have to wrap a towel and humiliate myself by knocking on the door of the adjoining room. He (hopefully not she!) could use the phone to call someone to enter my room and let me back in. I knocked at the door of the other room. No answer. A little louder knock, but still no answer. I knew he wasn't in the bathroom, because I was. There was obviously no one in that room. Now I was really stuck.

What to do? I could wait in the room for the maid to come, but that could be hours. I could yell until someone heard and came to the rescue, but they might not be able to hear me. Or I could simply break open that miserable door, which should have been more foolproof (I use the term advisedly) anyway.

Have you ever actually tried to break open a door? It is not as easy as it looks on television, especially when you are trying to do it with a bare shoulder. One lunge and the door simply shuddered. I was too timid. A second try, this time with gusto, and the frame gave way. Freedom! A few splinters lay on the floor, but I was liberated from the loo!

When I checked out of the room, I mentioned to the clerk that the door frame had been broken and would need some attention. He just looked at me and said not a word. It appeared I was not the first.

Occasionally, form becomes distorted, function breaks down, and the process of life seems to come to a halt. Due to difficult experiences of life, we could find ourselves locked in an emotionally imprisoning room from which easy exit should be available but isn't. We may feel naked, abandoned, and desperate, with no hope of rescue. We might knock on the doors of others, hoping for answers, but not a soul appears. We may sit waiting, hoping for someone to discover us when they come to clean up the mess we have made, but no one comes. In near panic, we could even try to break down the barriers, but find that bare hands and shoulders are sometimes not strong enough. What a lonely and frightening feeling!

The temptation can be great to succumb to that potentially overwhelming feeling. But remember, it is only a feeling. As difficult as it may be to believe in the moment of desperation, the architect of your life (which in reality is you!) has simply designed false doors or ancient locks. Both can be overcome.

When illusionary doorways appear to be impenetrable, there are true exits and actual entrances through which you can come and go for relief, for answers, and for new ideas that lead to positive solutions. In the style of Indiana Jones, you can find the hidden passageway that will set you free to pursue a more meaningful path. The lock may be old and the mechanism poorly designed, but you just have to find the right combination, the correct set of keys, and things will open up for you.

Remember, too, that even though you feel abandoned, there truly are others available and willing to help. No screaming required, just a simple request for assistance. You may have to be patient and persistent, but they will eventually be there. Family, friends, and others will reach out to help you unlock the doors, or open the windows, or make new exits, if needed.

Once you are free, learn from the experience. Understand emotional locks and dead-end doorways. Pay attention so you do not get stuck in the future. Then dress yourself, go out and find someone who is in the same predicament, and help set that person free.

If you never find yourself locked in, you can watch and listen for those who are and lend a caring hand. Sometimes all it takes is a simple turning of the key by someone on the right side of the door.

No situation is so desperate, no circumstance so severe, that eventual relief is not possible. False doorways are sometimes placed for our learning

and experience, and even for our edification.
Faulty locks provide opportunity for discovery of
useful keys. These represent stepping stones along
the learning path that leads to a life well lived.

*Around, over, or through,
there is always a way out.*

A Peaceful Place

I'm sure my parents received the announcement of an impending hurricane with little enthusiasm, but for me, a boy of eleven, it was tremendously exciting. The menacing storm had crawled along just off the eastern coast of the United States as far north as New Jersey and was turning onto the land. Now the hurricane was headed directly for our small town of Toms River.

It was summer, so there was no school, and I just stayed around home waiting for the storm to hit. The sky was overcast. The feeling of anticipation was electric. Preparations of window taping, battery changing, and water storing made it all the more dramatic.

Then the wind began to blow. Just a breeze at first, but it soon became a mighty, howling beast that drove the raindrops like bullets and took up, if it could, anything not tied down.

I stationed myself out on the big porch of our house just out of the rain and watched as the forces of nature unraveled. A garbage can clanged down the street like a tin can pulled behind some newly-weds' jalopy. Lightning, thunder, broken tree limbs, and flying debris—wow, what a great storm!

After a while the wind seemed to die down rather suddenly. There were a few breaks in the clouds. The patches of blue sky, the birds singing, and the now-soft breeze almost made me forget about the natural disaster that only minutes before had been ravaging our neighborhood. It was peaceful and beautiful, a calm beyond calm. It was the eye of the hurricane.

It didn't take long for me to realize that the pace would pick up again before we were through with this windy, rainy struggle, and, sure enough, the full force of the hurricane was back upon us in short order. Round one, a bit of a breather, and now round two.

Thank goodness there was no knockout

punch! Actually, I enjoyed the whole thing, from start to finish, but I think the town felt a little beat up when the storm finally passed for good.

Sometimes our lives are a lot like that storm. The winds of stress and pressure blow hard. Work, family, and other responsibilities send all kinds of things clanging across our path, great challenges to our intellectual preparation, emotional stability, and physical resistance. Life can be incredibly fun, but we do sometimes feel a little beat up.

How nice to realize that there is for each of us a place where the blue sky shines through, the birds sing, and the soft breezes blow. There's a quiet place deep down inside of us, away from the storm. Here we can find a brief reprieve from the daily disaster. All we have to do is learn to go there from time to time. We can enjoy a refreshing calm that will strengthen us against the onslaught that, just like the other half of the hurricane, surely must descend upon us.

A quiet place, a quiet mind, a comfortable chair, and a pleasant thought. Hold that thought. If it escapes, quietly bring it back. It will stay a little longer this time. A bit of practice and you can go to the eye of your personal hurricane whenever you need to. Just knowing it is there can often be comfort enough.

Even in the roughest weather, a calm center awaits with rest and comfort.

20

A One-Eyed Pony

He was a good enough looking horse—a little small, but adequately stout to do the job. My friend and the pony's owner, Tiny (his name belied his stature), assured me that this horse would have no trouble negotiating our rugged trail. So, saddle well installed, I climbed on. The horse refused to move.

We were in the bottom of the Grand Canyon at the village of Supai, the ancestral home of the Havasupai tribe. It was an eight-mile trek out of the canyon, and riding seemed the superior way to make it to the top. This Indian pony had been over the trail many times, I suppose. That's probably why he wasn't anxious to go through it again, especially with me on his back. But, with a lot of frustrated cajoling and the help of a small switch used to tickle his tail, my horse began to walk slowly up the trail.

At the outskirts of the village we reached a small bridge. The pony acted like this was the point of no return. If he went across the bridge, going up the trail must have seemed to him to be inevitable. So he stopped again.

This horse had a mind of his own and he was not the least bit interested in a long walk with 170 pounds on his back. I promised him cool water and fresh oats at the end of the trail. He didn't move a muscle. I spoke to him of the long and mutually beneficial relationship of man and the beast of burden. He was not impressed. Tiny finally cut a bigger stick.

I think the pony knew we wouldn't beat him, but he must have figured I was of such a base mentality that reason would never alter my determination to ride. We set off at a leisurely pace. A pace determined wholly by my sturdy mount.

I admit ashamedly that we did use the switch on his flanks a time or two in utter frustration. It made absolutely no difference. His gait, with the slow rhythm of a funeral dirge, never quickened. I could have walked twice as fast as he was willing to carry me.

Ultimately, I guess he got sick and tired of carrying me at all. With no warning, my unfaithful pony bolted up a steep incline at the side of the trail and I went rolling backwards off the saddle, heels over head, into a heap on the ground. Tiny laughed. "He always does that when he gets a little spooked. You know," he said, "he can only see out of the one eye, so he spooks easily." Well, now I was spooked, even with two good eyes. I rode on Tiny's horse the rest of the way out of the canyon.

In the end, the one-eyed pony got his cool water and fresh oats. I had a reasonably pleasant trip to the canyon rim, and all was well.

I learned something from this experience. It was summed up well by the writer of that old proverb, "You can lead a horse to water, but you can't make him drink." You can also lead a horse to the trail head, but you can't make him walk any faster than he wants to. I don't think we humans are much different once we learn we have the power.

Unless overpowering physical or psychological force is used, usually in a violent fashion, no one can make us do anything we don't want to do. We have the power to determine our own behavior. We lose the power only by giving it up.

My little children often blamed their less-than-noble behavior on a sibling or some other source of irresistible motivation. "He (or she) made me do it," they would say, as if they had absolutely no choice in the matter. In reality, nearly all of what we do, we do by choice. To the parents goes the responsibility of teaching the children that no one can *make* them do anything.

This is particularly true when it comes to feelings. Someone might be able to physically force us to do something we don't want to do. They would, however, be very hard pressed to make us feel something we're determined not to feel. We can't be forced into a feeling. Sorry, kids, nobody can *make* you mad.

We seem to have developed a habit in our modern world of relinquishing our personal power. We seem to quite easily let someone else decide what we should do or how we should feel. A vivid example of this is so-called "road rage." At the careless turn of a steering wheel or the thoughtless flash of a rude gesture, we may let some person (oops, I almost said *idiot*) determine how we're going to feel or act.

"Road rage" is almost instantaneous. How quickly we surrender our personal power! In a split second we might react with our own rude gesture and then blame it on the other driver, when all the while we really acted of our own volition. It seems much easier and safer to just ignore the rudeness of others or, better yet, attribute it to ignorance or just a simple mistake. No sense getting upset over a simple mistake.

So, sure, the one-eyed Indian pony won. I couldn't make him carry me out of the canyon the way I wanted him to. He decided to keep his personal power and not yield it to me. But I decided to keep mine, too. That horse couldn't *make* me mad and he couldn't *make* me resent his stubbornness. Hey, maybe we both won.

No one can take your personal power. It can only be surrendered.

(21)

Say What?

When we send our children off to school, we can, for the most part, have a high degree of confidence that they will receive an adequate educational experience. The teachers are usually dedicated, have a reasonable understanding of the course material, and certainly have in mind the best interests of the students. I am grateful for the corps of educators who guided my years of formal learning and gave so much to my own children as they walked the sometimes tedious but often exciting pathway of public education.

The best teachers seem to be those who communicate to both the mind and the heart of the student. I'm remembering, for example, Miss Thompson. (It was really *Mrs.*, and yes, I was a disappointed nine-year-old when I learned she had another man in her life.) She not only taught me the wonder and power of reading but also empowered me as a person. By allowing me to keep a pet white rat in my desk during the day, and by providing an aquarium for the pollywogs we caught at the pond, she sent the message that even our childish notions could be made meaningful and become learning experiences. In that case, I learned that cleaning up after a white rat that has spent all day in a desk is not particularly pleasant.

I had another teacher who ranted and raved to control the class and seemed bent on making each of her students afraid of her. She sent a message as well. She appeared to be telling us that education was not supposed to be fun and that if you wanted to have a good time you had to do it surreptitiously, when you thought you would not be caught in the useless act. I have only vague memories of that year and can't even remember the teacher's name. I guess I'm in a sort of denial that such a school year ever occurred in my life.

Obviously, to take full advantage of our educational experiences does require a great deal of effort. Learning seems to offer almost equal doses of joyous epiphany and downright toil and drudgery. We need to work up a few good brain calluses if we really want to get a powerful grip on the subject matter.

But in addition to discipline, an emotionally warm environment is necessary for the incubation of good ideas and for healthy educational development. Sometimes a deficit in academic excellence on the part of a teacher can even be offset by the fact that he or she really cares about the students.

An educator with whom we spent many years as our children, one by one, rung by rung, climbed the elementary school ladder was outstanding in his attitude even though his own intellectual prowess was less than razor sharp. He created a climate for successful learning despite the fact that he may have appeared to some to be less than learned himself. He was kind of a down-home guy for whom dressing for success meant nothing more than clean and modest clothing. For him, the English language was easy because he did not worry about the conjugation of many of the verbs.

"To see," for example, was used in only one form, regardless of the subject or tense, as in, "I know he's here, I seen him." Or, "We seen that movie and they seen it with us!" He spent so little energy worrying about grammar that he could devote more than usual effort caring for the pupils in his devoted charge.

At first his grammar grated on our ears as if he were scouring the chalkboard with overgrown fingernails, but it didn't take long to realize that he was a master at creating an atmosphere of exciting discovery. We could teach good grammar at home. The lack of it at school was a small price to pay for the lasting benefit of a schoolroom in which a nurturing teacher worked his magic and grew the minds and hearts of his young scholars.

These days the idea of mentors has really caught on. To have a dedicated mentor is like hooking your wagon to a rocket. Such a personal guru will guide and inspire and very often help to flatten the steepest learning curve. One such person once said to me, "I can teach you in five weeks what it took me five years to learn, because no one was there to guide me." He did. I still had to put my newfound knowledge into disciplined practice, but my practice could come much closer to perfection as a result of his beneficent tutelage.

There is a certain triteness to the saying, *I don't care how much you know until I know how much you care.* But there is also a great deal of truth in that well-worn proverb. When we hear a person slaughter the King's English, we might recoil and think to ourselves, "Say what?" But if we listen carefully and see beyond the grammar, we may be in for a learning treat. I know, I done it once or twice.

People learn best what they are taught with love.

22

Those Who Sing Best

Some time ago my family and I went on a short vacation over a long holiday weekend. Some wonderful friends invited us to their cabin near Lake Tahoe. This beautiful Sierra mountain setting provided a peaceful yet exciting place to rest a little, play a little, and take some time to renew our perspective on life. We needed to have some fun. The "Jack" in me was becoming a "dull boy."

One afternoon we wandered through an art fair, visually sampling the wares of talented artists and artisans. Contemplating the exquisitely hand-carved birds, well-thrown pots, and perfectly framed paintings and photographs provided an almost spiritual experience. Besides being incredibly talented, most of these vendors of art had obviously put heart and soul into their creations.

After seeing what we could, we boarded a little shuttle bus for a ride back to the cabin. Another family boarded with us. They appeared to be three generations—grandparents, children, and grandchildren—out for the same rich experience we had enjoyed. Everyone was in a good mood, so it came naturally to sing along to the Beatles tune that was blaring a little too loudly from the speakers mounted in the ceiling of the bus.

It wasn't a contest, but it seemed the louder we sang, the louder the other family sang. The grandparents seemed to know the song the best, but the children were definitely getting into it by the time the song ended. The grandkids were a little too young to join in, but offered smiling approval of their parents' attempt to harmonize with McCartney and Lennon.

Soon the bus stopped, and the three generations clambered off. As she entered the doorway of the bus, Grandma turned, looked at us with a pixie grin, and said, "Those who sing best get off first." Before we could reply she was gone, just leaving us to think of what we might have said and didn't. She won.

Soon after we arrived back at the cabin, I received a telephone call that caused my light-heartedness to dissolve quickly into sadness. A good friend, only recently diagnosed with a life-threatening illness, had suddenly passed away. He was a relatively young man and truly in his professional prime. Just a few weeks before, he had seemed so vital and enthusiastic about his work, his family, and his faith. He was gone too early.

It brought back memories of my father, who died of cancer at age fifty-six. He had so looked forward to the retirement he almost lived to see. My father was as good a man as ever there was and didn't deserve to go at such an early age. Nor did my mother deserve his departure from this life and the companionless years that lay ahead for her.

I thought of the daughter of some dear friends, taken in her fresh-faced adolescence. I remembered a beautiful baby boy, placed in the arms of a loving adoptive couple. They had waited so long for him to come into their family. The next time I saw him, he was lying in the silk folds of a tiny casket.

It often seems that the most wonderful, the most innocent, the most beautiful people are taken from us before we are at all ready to let them go. Sometimes, those who sing best get off first, leaving us thinking of things we might have said and didn't. They win.

Time doesn't dictate the fullness of a life. Sometimes life is shortest for the best of us.

(23)

Throwing Stones

Parents and their rebellious children often go through a tragic repetition of hostile confrontations, destructive yelling matches, and, occasionally, actual physical battles. These are accompanied on both sides by demoralizing feelings of rejection and failure. The more such devastating scenes are played out, the worse things seem to become, and the greater grows the distance between the frustrated parents and the struggling child.

I recall a circumstance plaguing a good family. They were doing their best to be close and to foster helpful communication, but everything that had worked with the other children was failing miserably for one teenage daughter. She flouted family values, openly challenged parental authority, frequently lied, and disobeyed even the most reasonable expectations of her parents. She stole money and other things of value to her mom and dad, even things she couldn't use. She didn't seem to be self-destructive or into drugs or that kind of thing, but a virtual war was being waged in that home between a teenager in crisis and her confused and grieving parents.

Ultimately, they decided to seek some guidance on what they might do to deal more effectively with the situation. Nothing else was working, so they gave me a call.

After speaking with the parents, I was pleased to learn that the young woman was willing to visit with me also. Willingness to talk to someone who wants to help is a real sign of maturity and of a sincere desire to make things better.

This confused young teen—I'll call her Sarah— was not immediately ready to share her feelings openly. We had to get to know each other, and she needed to feel some trust that I wouldn't betray her. What she didn't need was another "parent" to tell her what to do or lecture her about how things ought to be. What she wanted most was a listening ear and a caring heart. Both were offered.

It didn't take long to realize that Sarah was really a fine person with a great desire to be successful in life. She understood right from wrong and knew that some of her behavior fell well within the latter category. She was smart, so why the acting out? What better way to find out than to ask?

"So, Sarah, you've had all this trouble with your parents. Things haven't been going well for you lately. I can think of several reasons why this might be happening. Do you mind if I share a few of them with you? Then you could tell me if I'm beginning to understand where you're coming from."

"Okay, I guess."

Now I was on the spot. How might she be feeling? What might be going on with her that I remembered happening to me when I was her age? One thing I knew: Even when young people can't identify their own feelings, they can at least confirm what feelings they are having if someone else articulates them. I would go fishing.

"Sarah, it's common for people your age to feel angry and hateful toward their parents. Are you feeling that way?"

"No, not really. They bug me, but I know they love me," she said with a shrug of her shoulders.

No bite. Wrong bait.

"I'm glad. So you feel okay about your parents?"

"Yes."

"Then why are you acting out against them so much?"

Oops. Remember, teenagers can confirm what they're feeling, but most of the time they can neither identify their feelings nor explain why they're doing what they're doing, so it doesn't really help to ask.

"Never mind that question," I said, backpedaling. "Maybe you're like a lot of other kids who are having a hard time in school and you feel frustrated and burned-out?"

I wanted to give her permission to feel

whatever she was feeling, to let her know that whatever it was, there were probably lots of others feeling that way, too. She was normal.

"No," she replied. "I like school."

Wrong bait again. I needed to look back into my own teenage memory.

"You know, Sarah, one of the hardest things for most people in your time of life is just dealing with fear. Not the spookhouse kind of fright, but a general fear of what's happening to them in life. You're getting older, and you may be feeling some of the fear and pressure that come with the thoughts of getting into college, leaving home, and being out on your own. There are hard decisions to make, and it all may feel kind of overwhelming. Have you been feeling some of that kind of fear?"

Sarah looked at me with a how-did-you-know gaze and nodded her head. "Yes," she said quietly and lowered her eyes.

It was easy to sense her fear and pain.

"I bet that's tough." And I remembered just how tough it could be.

We talked some more, and she shared her

concerns about the future and how she would ever measure up. No sermons were necessary. No "buck up, you can do it" lectures. Just a little caring, a little understanding. She knew she'd been heard, and that was the most important thing.

As soon as I could, I met with her parents and offered them a little illustration of what seemed to be happening between them and their daughter.

Imagine a beautiful beach with warm, white sand and a few palm trees swaying in the gentle breeze. The temperature is perfect. The azure water is washing softly onto the shore. The beach is deserted except for one little family. Just a mom and dad and their teenage daughter.

The folks are relaxing, even dozing, on a blanket on the sand while their daughter strolls along the beach picking up stones. She is fascinated by the pebbles, which have been rounded and smoothed through years of delicate abrasion, pushed against the sand by the water. She has found several worth keeping and holds them tightly in her hand.

The girl can't swim, but she is old enough to

know not to go in over her head, so her parents are not worried about her. Interestingly, she has been mute since birth, she has never spoken, so she isn't even making noise to disturb her parents. They are not paying any attention to her as they soak up the sun and enjoy their rest.

As the small waves wash up around her ankles, the young girl takes a few adventurous steps farther out into the surf, just to see what it's like. She is jostled a bit by the waves, but her feet never leave the sand at the bottom, and she is in no danger. A little farther out. No harm; she can still touch bottom. The water is only up to her chest. A little larger wave lifts her off her feet, but it passes, and she gently settles back down.

After a few minutes of this game, a big wave rolls in. This one really picks the girl up, moves her several feet, and sets her down directly over a hole in the ocean floor. She isn't far from shore, but the water is way over her head as she drops below the surface straining to make contact with something solid.

Panic comes on her quickly as she realizes she

is in desperate trouble. She can't swim, so she is thrashing about. No one is paying attention. She can't speak. Her fear erupts only in a silent scream. No one can hear her. Down she sinks.

With all her might she pushes off the bottom and surfaces for just a second. A gasp for air and then, without thinking, she takes one of the stones in her hand and throws it with all her might in the direction of her oblivious parents. Driven with force and accuracy far beyond her natural ability, the stone hits her father right in the head. Up from the blanket he comes, angry and in pain.

Blinded by the sun and the sharp pang in his head, he yells some angry warning in the direction he last saw his daughter and lies back down on the blanket. What is the matter with that girl!

Down she goes again into the foaming water. Again, with all her might, using up the last of her strength she kicks off the bottom and raises up just high enough to allow her to throw one more stone of horrified chance. Once again, driven with force and accuracy far beyond her natural ability, the stone hits her father right in the head. This time he is up and running, stunned and angry, bound to stop this painful nonsense.

As his eyes adjust to the brightness, he sees his daughter's dire position. Quickly he wades into the water and pulls her to the safety of the shore. Within moments, Mom and Dad measure her condition and find that their dear daughter is fine. She is frightened and not at all anxious to go back into the water, but she is okay.

The girl in the story desperately needed her parents' attention. She was drowning, but she couldn't call out. All she could do was throw stones to communicate her plight, hoping they would see her need and respond with a rescue.

The parents of the rebellious teenager with whom I talked recognized immediately the circumstance of their daughter. She was drowning in the sea of life, frightened nearly to death of the future and full of panic, flailing about for something solid. She didn't know how to communicate her plight. She had never been able to really talk to her parents. All she could seem to do was throw rocks at the only ones she knew would never reject or abandon her.

At first they reacted only to the almost blinding pain caused by her behavior. They were angry and screamed a warning. Finally, they felt more concern for her than for their own discomfort. They were then able to really pay attention and come to her rescue.

Mom and Dad began to truly listen to their daughter. They began to hear her. She no longer felt the need to throw stones. They had lots of work to do, much to learn about each other and to practice as they worked things out, but the fear and anger were replaced with love and hope and appreciation.

Children can't "throw stones" at their friends. They will be rejected rapidly. They can't strike out at their teachers. They'll usually just be disciplined and labeled. They have to communicate their unspoken dread to those who represent unqualified love and acceptance. This kind of acting out is kind of a back-handed compliment to Mom and Dad or some other faithful soul, but it represents a child-like trust that should really be appreciated.

Young people would most likely be glad simply to talk about their problems, but they struggle to put into words just how they really feel. Ask a teenager how he or she feels and all you're going to get is the shoulder-shrug routine and an "I don't know."

So, the next time someone you love, especially one of the kids, throws a figurative stone at you, by all means duck, but then deal quickly with the behavior and pay most of your attention to why he or she threw it. Fewer stones will be thrown, not as many people will drown in the quagmire of life, and you won't have so many knots on your head.

Those who throw stones need a lifeline, not a lecture.

(24)

The Man in the Mirror

The story is told of a man who was asked to deliver an important address to a prestigious audience. For him, it was a most significant opportunity to convey what he considered to be a vital message to a group of people who would be greatly benefited in hearing it. As he gave the talk, he sensed a certain uneasiness in the audience. He couldn't seem to capture their full attention. Some let their gaze wander about the room, others looked down at their feet, and a few seemed lost in their day planners. So many were focusing on anything but him that he became more animated in his presentation in an attempt to win their interest. He raised his voice, he gestured more broadly, he even tried to be funny, but got nowhere. The harder he tried, the fewer people who seemed to be listening, and some of them were even smiling at him in a curious way.

At the end of the speech, he felt like a miserable failure. People were courteous but would not engage him in conversation or show much interest in discussing the merits of his presentation. The audience quickly dissipated, and the frustrated speaker made his way to the rest room near the meeting place. As he entered the rest room, he happened to glance in the mirror. To his great dismay, the man who looked back at him in the glass presented a most humorous sight. The tie he had tucked behind the top button of his shirt to avoid any spillage at lunch was still crammed into its protective position. In his anxiety over the speech, he had failed to notice that he looked less like a distinguished lecturer and more like an unmade bed. No wonder the audience didn't want to look at him. He groaned and in dejection said out loud to no one in particular, "If only I had looked in a mirror before I got up to speak! Why didn't someone tell me?" An opportunity was lost for want of a clear and honest reflection.

Though that particular story is most likely fictional, many people have suffered similar experiences because no one was kind enough to let them know about some minor problem that rendered them almost completely ineffective. From a crooked tie to a tooth adorned with spinach to some sort of behavior that is out of place for the setting, we all occasionally suffer from some form of temporary dishevelment. All it takes to set us straight is someone who will hold up a virtual mirror and verbally reflect their own view of the matter so we can correct the little deficit. But most people are unwilling to point out the problem.

Like sponges, we tend to absorb what we see in another person, unwilling to let loose of our observation and fearful to mention something that obviously needs a little fixing. We seem to be more concerned about ourselves and how we might be thought of in the situation than we are of the poor, uninformed person who will ultimately learn of his or her misfortune. At that point, long after we might have been helpful, the individual will likely feel embarrassed and perhaps even betrayed by those who could have saved the day and didn't. Perhaps there are too few mirrors in the world and too many sponges.

It is interesting to note the difference between the function of a mirror and that of a sponge. The sponge is designed to soak up and retain whatever comes its way. It releases its contents only when someone puts the squeeze on it and it is forced to let go. A mirror, on the other hand, is built to reflect what it sees, to offer back a true representation of all it is offered. Without coercion, a mirror can provide real and immediate feedback, usually limited solely by the inclination of the viewer to accurately assess the image.

Mirrors can, however, become addictive. There is a temptation to self-appraise frequently with a glance in the glass of another person's eye. Unchecked, this can become an obsessive need to examine our position constantly and to gauge our worth by the assumed valuation of others. This creates a serious risk of a confused and ever-shifting sense of reality.

It is important to remember, also, that we may come across people who are only too willing to offer their candid opinion of how things are. Such people generally consider themselves to be frank and open and honest, really "telling it like it is." But their viewpoint may be warped and skewed by selfishness, jealousy, or misunderstanding. The image they offer may be no more accurate than that of a fun-house mirror and should be taken no more seriously. We wouldn't comb our hair or judge the look of our smile by focusing on the slithering, wavy image of the circus looking glass or the bulging, bloated reflection in the carnival midway mirror. Nor should we pay undue attention to the false likeness by which some would have us judge ourselves. If the image portrayed by someone else just doesn't seem to fit, we ought to set aside our fears of the truth, seek out a trusted confidant, and test out the possibilities with a second opinion.

I will never forget, though it happened when I was just a young boy, the look on the face of a fine man when I revealed to him the unfortunate criticism of a thoughtless gossip. He was not angry with me, the simple-minded message bearer, nor was he upset with the one who spoke unkindly behind his back. But even now I can sense the way he focused on the untruth and, with a choking gulp, swallowed the lie. Subsequent events proved he had fed upon many misrepresentations of himself until he could no longer see the real man, so good and of such great value. Oh, the harm of a long-term poisoning of one's self-image!

As we develop our ability to offer a helpful reflection to those around us, it is good to grow, also, in our sense of balance. Wisdom and experience dictate when to absorb in the manner of a sponge and when to hold up the mirror of personal observation. Too much of either one can be equally damaging. When we have honed our interpersonal skills and are motivated by love and a real desire to help, we will know just how much to hold and the right amount to show. We will then become an invaluable asset to those around us.

People who truly seek the well-being of those who walk with them through life will learn by love

to give what is needed to make the trek more pleasant and productive. Thus will the joy of the passage increase.

True reflection will guide
our adjustment to life.

About the Author

Don H. Staheli holds a bachelor's degree in history and master's degrees in international management and social work. He has assisted thousands of people in his work as a licensed psychotherapist and trainer, and is currently a full-time administrator. He is the author of the bestselling children's book *The Story of the Walnut Tree*. Don and his wife, Cyndy, have five children and six grandchildren and live in Bountiful, Utah.